Benedetto

MARCELLO

CONCERTO

In C Minor

FOR OBOE AND PIANO

K 04515

CONCERTO

BENEDETTO MARCELLO
(1686-1739)

BELWIN/MILLS PUBLISHING CORP.

K–4515

A *Kalmus Classic Edition*

Benedetto

MARCELLO

CONCERTO

In C Minor

OBOE

K 04515

CONCERTO

OBOE

Allegro moderato (♪ = 104)

BENEDETTO MARCELLO
(1686-1739)

OBOE